Be the Change! Shaping Your Community

Be a CONSERVATIONIST!

By Matt Jankowski

Gareth Stevens PUBLISHING

Please visit our website, www.garethstevens.com. For a free color catalog of all our high-quality books, call toll free 1-800-542-2595 or fax 1-877-542-2596.

Cataloging-in-Publication Data

Names: Jankowski, Matt.
Title: Be a conservationist! / Matt Jankowski.
Description: New York : Gareth Stevens Publishing, 2019. | Series: Be the change! shaping your community | Includes index.
Identifiers: LCCN ISBN 9781538220054 (pbk.) | ISBN 9781538220030 (library bound) | ISBN 9781538220061 (6 pack)
Subjects: LCSH: Nature conservation–Juvenile literature. | Environmentalism–Juvenile literature. | Environmental protection–Citizen participation–Juvenile literature. | Nature conservation–Citizen participation–Juvenile literature.
Classification: LCC GE195.5 J36 2018 | DDC 363.7092'53–dc23
First Edition

Published in 2019 by
Gareth Stevens Publishing
111 East 14th Street, Suite 349
New York, NY 10003

Designer: Laura Bowen
Editor: Joan Stoltman

Photo credits: Cover, p. 1 (main) wavebreakmedia/Shutterstock.com; cover, p. 1 (background) Dmitry Naumov/Shutterstock.com; p. 4 buradaki/Shutterstock.com; p. 5 Mint Images - Frans Lanting/Mint Images/Getty Images; p. 7 kali9/E+/Getty Images; p. 9 JHU Sheridan Libraries/Gado/Contributor/Archive Photos/Getty Images; p. 10 XXLPhoto/Shutterstock.com; p. 11 JODY AMIET/Stringer/AFP/Getty Images; p. 12 Karel Cerny/Shutterstuck.com; p. 13 (frog) MriMan/Shutterstock.com; p. 13 (shark) Danler/Shutterstock.com; p. 13 (giraffe) Zhenyakot/Shutterstock.com; pp. 14–15 KidStock/Blend Images/Getty Images; p. 17 Paul Simcock/Corbis/Getty Images; p. 19 Justin Sullivan/Stringer/Getty Images North America/Getty Images; p. 21 Rich Carey/Shutterstock.com; p. 23 Patrizio Martorana/Shutterstock.com; p. 25 plantic/Shutterstock.com; p. 26 Andrey_Popov/Shutterstock.com; p. 27 Design Pics/Kristy-Anne Glubish/Getty Images; p. 29 Dmytro Zinkevych/Shutterstock.com.

Printed in the United States of America

CPSIA compliance information: Batch #CS18GS: For further information contact Gareth Stevens, New York, New York at 1-800-542-2595.

CONTENTS

Words in the glossary appear in **bold** type the first time they are used in the text.

Our Precious Home

Earth is our home, which means it's our job to take care of it! But of the billions of people living here, not everyone is concerned with the state of the planet. Pollution, the waste of **natural resources**, and the overhunting of animals all harm Earth and its **ecosystems**. That's why conservation is important!

Conservation is caring for and protecting the natural world. People who purposely work to take care of our planet are called conservationists. They may work to protect animals, plants, water, or areas of land. Does this sound like work you'd like to do, too? Become a conservationist today!

Clean and Safe

Humans live in all kinds of **environments** on Earth. Keeping the places where we live clean and safe is important for our health as well as the health of animals and plants. Pollution, for example, can make drinking water unsafe! Polluted water can make people, animals, and plants very sick.

Pangolins are the most poached, or illegally hunted, animal on Earth. Over 1 million pangolins may have been poached since 2007! Conservationists are working hard to save their **species** from dying out.

Being a Conservationist

The coolest part about conservation is that it's something anyone can do! Teachers, truck drivers, chefs, and people with any other job can spend their spare time **volunteering** to support environmental causes they care about.

Some people are **professional** conservationists! Their job may be to work right in nature planting trees, helping hurt animals, or cleaning up polluted areas with special tools. They may also teach people about conservation by holding classes, giving speeches, or working with companies and governments to help them do business in ways that are safer for the environment. Many conservationists spend time raising money for projects and **research**.

Your Turn!

If you're thinking about becoming a conservationist, you probably love and respect nature and wildlife. Professional conservationists often have special skills—such as working with tools, taking pictures, writing, researching, or teaching—that they put to use helping Earth. These are all skills you can start working on today!

These people are cleaning a neighborhood park in their spare time because they know it's important to keep our planet clean. You can volunteer to clean up your local park, too!

The History of Conservation

The conservation movement started in the United States around the 1850s. By the late 1800s, laws that protected certain animals and turned certain areas of land into national parks were being passed. In 1901, Theodore Roosevelt was elected president. He loved nature and passed laws protecting three times more forests!

As the 1900s went on, conservation laws grew to include limits on hunting and fishing. People began to understand how important clean air and water were to human health, too. Laws about these matters, as well as about protecting endangered animals, or animals in danger of dying out, continue to be passed today.

A Long Problem

From cutting down big parts of rain forests to dumping waste into rivers, people have been harming Earth for hundreds of years. They continue to do so today. Even if everyone started acting like a conservationist, it would take many years to fix the problems Earth already has!

Scientist Rachel Carson wrote the book *Silent Spring* about the harm caused by pest-killing chemicals called pesticides. More than 2 million copies have been sold since 1962. Many people agree that Carson's book started the modern environmental movement.

Today, one of the biggest conservation groups in the world is the International Union for Conservation of Nature (IUCN). IUCN studies the state of the natural world. More than 1,300 member groups from over 170 countries are part of IUCN! Together, they work to protect animals and areas of land from harm. They also support Earth-friendly laws and policies, or rules.

Climate change is one area IUCN is working on in many ways. They're studying how climate change affects animals, forests, and oceans. IUCN also supports member groups around the world working on climate change issues, such as keeping coastal areas healthy.

climate change

Climate change is the slow warming of Earth due to people's activities. Burning fossil fuels, pollution, and even certain kinds of livestock farming all contribute to climate change. Because of climate change, Earth's seas are rising, storms are becoming worse and happening more often, and average temperatures are getting hotter!

These scientists are studying mangroves. Mangroves are plants in coastal ecosystems that may be greatly affected by climate change.

Another of the biggest conservation groups is the World Wildlife Fund (WWF). WWF raises money and works with people and groups around the world to keep water clean, protect animals, and more. Nearly 5 million members around the world support WWF.

The WWF is best known for helping endangered species. They have a program anyone can join where people can "adopt" a species in need of help. You and your family or class at school can choose from a list of animals, including pandas and tigers, and send money that goes toward the WWF's efforts to save Earth.

It's Time for Change!

IUCN was founded in 1948. The WWF was founded in 1961. Even though they have millions of people working toward protecting Earth, they haven't been around long enough to undo all the harm that's already been done. However, they're loud voices of conservation that are often heard today!

POPULATION PROBLEMS

DROP IN POPULATION FROM 1970 TO 2012

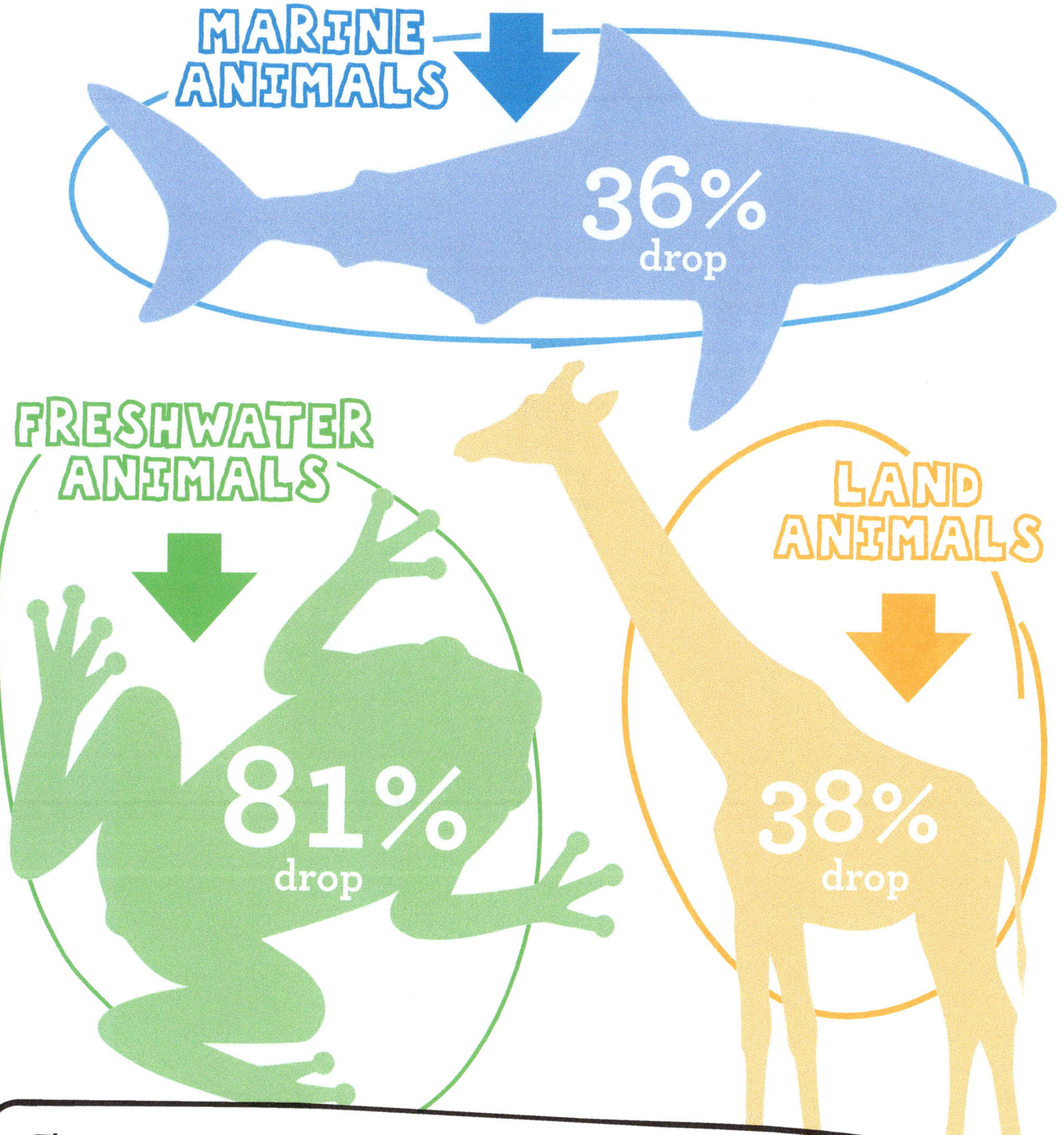

The Living Planet Report is a paper published every 2 years by the WWF about Earth's continued need for conservation. The 2016 report showed that there had been major drops in animal populations between 1970 and 2012.

Find a Group!

Your school is a great place to get started as a conservationist. By joining a conservation club, you can meet other kids who care about the environment and work on projects to help the world around you right now. You could plant trees near your school, clean up a park, or have a bake sale to raise money for the WWF! If a conservation club doesn't exist at your school, start one!

Your Turn!

Another way you can get started as a conservationist is to spread your message! Wear a T-shirt that supports something you care about, such as clean water. Do a school project on an endangered animal and present it to your class. There are many ways you can get the word out!

There are also many groups you could join, such as the Scouts, that often do conservation work. A local community center or library might host events about conservation, too.

There are many ways to get people in your community interested in conservation. Share your knowledge with your friends or ask your youth group or school to bring in speakers to raise awareness.

Types of Conservation

Environmental conservationists often work outside, studying land, water, and plants. They sometimes help clean up polluted areas of land and water. To learn more about the environment, they may collect samples of plants, rocks, and soil that will go to a laboratory for research. They may even run the laboratory!

Environmental conservationists use their knowledge of science and nature to protect the environment and human health. They can help governments understand nature, which in turn helps governments pass laws to protect it. Environmental conservationists also work with companies to reduce the amount of pollution and waste their factories create.

An Incredible Woman

Margaret Murie is known as the "grandmother of the conservation movement." She helped pass the 1964 Wilderness Act to protect 9.1 million acres (3.7 million ha) of land. She also helped create the Arctic National Wildlife Refuge, America's largest national wildlife refuge. A refuge is an area in which animals can safely live.

Conservationists need to be prepared before taking on a cleanup project. Plan ahead to make sure you have tools and supplies ready before your group gets started.

Wildlife Conservationists

Wildlife conservationists study animals in their ecosystems. They may track wild animals to learn about their movements and habits. Some wildlife conservationists study how climate change affects species and ecosystems. Still others work to pass laws and fight against illegal hunting of endangered species.

Wildlife conservationists often spend time in areas where disasters have occurred. Disasters are events that cause great suffering or loss. Some of these disasters, such as floods, are natural. Others, such as oil spills, are man-made. Wildlife conservationists clean animals affected by oil spills, rescue animals from dangerous situations, and heal hurt animals.

An Awesome Zoologist!

Jane Goodall is a zoologist best known for studying the behaviors of chimpanzees. Zoologists study animal life. Goodall is also an animal rights activist, which means she fights for animals to be treated kindly. She's received many honors. In 2002, the United Nations (UN) named her a Messenger of Peace.

Steve Irwin was a famous wildlife conservationist. He worked hard to educate people about animals. He had a popular TV show for years and also owned and operated the Australia Zoo until his death in 2006.

Marine Conservationists

Marine conservation is the protection and preservation of ocean ecosystems. Like other kinds of conservation, its goals are to repair areas that have already been hurt, stop further problems, and save endangered species from dying out. One of the biggest issues in this field today is saving coral reef ecosystems.

Marine conservation is important because the ocean covers more than 70 percent of Earth, and we've explored less than 5 percent of it! That means when people cause issues in the ocean with pollution and overfishing, not even marine scientists know what the real long-term effects will be.

He's Saving the Ocean!

Jean-Michel Cousteau is an ocean explorer and **environmentalist** from a family of ocean explorers and environmentalists. He started a group called the Ocean Futures Society to educate people about the sea. He's spread the message of marine conservation through more than 80 movies that he filmed by bringing video cameras underwater with him while diving!

Coral reefs are underwater hills made up of the hard parts of tiny sea animals. Reefs provide food, homes, and protection for millions of species. Marine conservationists are working hard to figure out how to protect and rebuild these ecosystems!

Freshwater Conservationists

In 2017, around 2.1 billion people lacked easy **access** to clean drinking water. Freshwater conservationists around the world are working to conserve and manage Earth's freshwater supply.

Water is naturally recycled, moving from Earth's surface, through the atmosphere, and falling back to Earth again as rain or snow. This means the amount of freshwater on Earth has always been about the same. Unfortunately, Earth's population has grown a lot over time, and people are using more freshwater than ever. Less than 1 percent of our planet's freshwater can easily be accessed, which means it's important for us to protect what little we have.

Your Turn!

You can save nearly 8 gallons (30 l) of water a day by turning off the water while brushing your teeth! You can also save water by taking showers instead of baths. A shower only uses 10 to 25 gallons (38 to 95 l) of water, while baths use up to 70 gallons (265 l)!

People and factories sometimes pollute water sources so badly they can't be cleaned or reused.

Garbage Everywhere!

People create over 1 billion tons (907 million mt) of garbage, or trash, each year. All this garbage sits in huge piles called landfills or dumps. Many of the things we throw away, such as plastics and metals, don't easily break down, so these piles just grow and grow!

One reason conservationists are concerned with growing landfill and dump sites is because they're often poorly built. That means toxins, or matter than is harmful, often drains into the soil and groundwater nearby. Toxins can end up in drinking water and soil used for growing food, causing health problems for animals and people.

Living with Garbage

In some parts of the world, people live right next to, or even in, landfills! There are even cities where people dump their garbage right into the streets or local water sources. Conservationists try to help people living in such conditions by finding them doctors, clean food, and homes in better areas.

Landfills and dumps are also big producers of greenhouse gases, or gases that get trapped in Earth's atmosphere and contribute to the warming of Earth.

Do Your Part!

Keeping garbage and pollution in check where you live is something you can help with! Be sure not to litter, and clean up other people's litter. Always recycle when you can, and help others recycle. **Donate** clothes, toys, and other things from around your house for other people to use instead of throwing them away.

Upcycling is the idea of taking something you could throw away and making it into something useful again. People have upcycled soup cans into flowerpots, boxes into toys, and even plastic bottles into brooms! Get together with your friends to see what ideas you can come up with!

In the United States, 30 to 40 percent of all food is thrown away each year. That's around 133 billion pounds (60 billion kg) of food!

Your Turn!

Talk to your parents about getting a recycling bin if you don't already have one. Sometimes you have to separate different kinds of recycling, so be sure to read the rules for your town. Offer to help your neighbors sort their recycling and bring it to the curb on pickup day.

Be Heard!

An important job for any conservationist is making their voice heard by those in government. Having government support for an environmental project can give conservation groups more money, people, and other resources to help them get a job done better and faster.

Is there a conservation issue in your town or state you'd like to see addressed? Send a letter or email to your mayor or congressperson! Sometimes, conservation problems are so big, laws are needed to fix them. With you on Earth's side, more of these laws may pass. There's no better time than now to speak up and protect our planet!

Your Turn!

If you want to do more as a conservationist when you get older, you can go to college for it! You can study environmental science or environmental law to have a direct **impact** on conservation. You can also travel around the world volunteering on many environmental projects!

CONSERVATION YOU CAN DO NOW!

To keep your neighborhood clean, join or start a club that picks up litter.

To prevent food waste, only buy or serve yourself as much food as you will eat.

To let your voice be heard, take part in a **protest** or march in support of the environment.

To prevent air pollution, plan ahead to ride along with friends.

Here are some ways to create change as a conservationist today!

GLOSSARY

access: the ability to use or enter something

donate: to give something to others who need it

ecosystem: all the living things in an area

environment: the conditions that surround a living thing and affect the way it lives; the natural world in which a plant or animal lives

environmentalist: someone who works to preserve, protect, and improve the natural world

impact: to have a strong effect on something

marine: the sea or the plants and animals that live in the sea

natural resource: something in nature that can be used by people

professional: having to do with a job that requires special skills, training, or education

protest: an event at which a group objects to an idea, an act, or a way of doing something

research: studying to find something new

species: a group of plants or animals that are all of the same kind

volunteer: to do work without being paid

FOR MORE INFORMATION

BOOKS

Baillie, Marilyn, Jonathan Baillie, and Ellen Butcher. *How to Save a Species.* Toronto, Canada: Owlkids Books, 2014.

Jankeliowitch, Anne. *Kids Who Are Changing The World.* Naperville, IL: Sourcebooks Jabberwocky, 2014.

Lundgren, Julie K. *How Do Humans Depend on Earth?* Vero Beach, FL: Rourke Educational Media, 2013.

WEBSITES

Earth Rangers
www.earthrangers.com
Learn more about saving animals and the environment and find out what it takes to become an Earth Ranger.

New York State Conservationist for Kids!
www.dec.ny.gov/education/105720.html
This site has lots of ideas for ways to reduce, reuse, and recycle as well as information about conservation issues all over the world.

USDA for Kids
www.usda.gov/our-agency/initiatives/usda-kids
The US Department of Agriculture's list of cool conservation websites for kids.

Publisher's note to educators and parents: Our editors have carefully reviewed these websites to ensure that they are suitable for students. Many websites change frequently, however, and we cannot guarantee that a site's future contents will continue to meet our high standards of quality and educational value. Be advised that students should be closely supervised whenever they access the internet.

INDEX